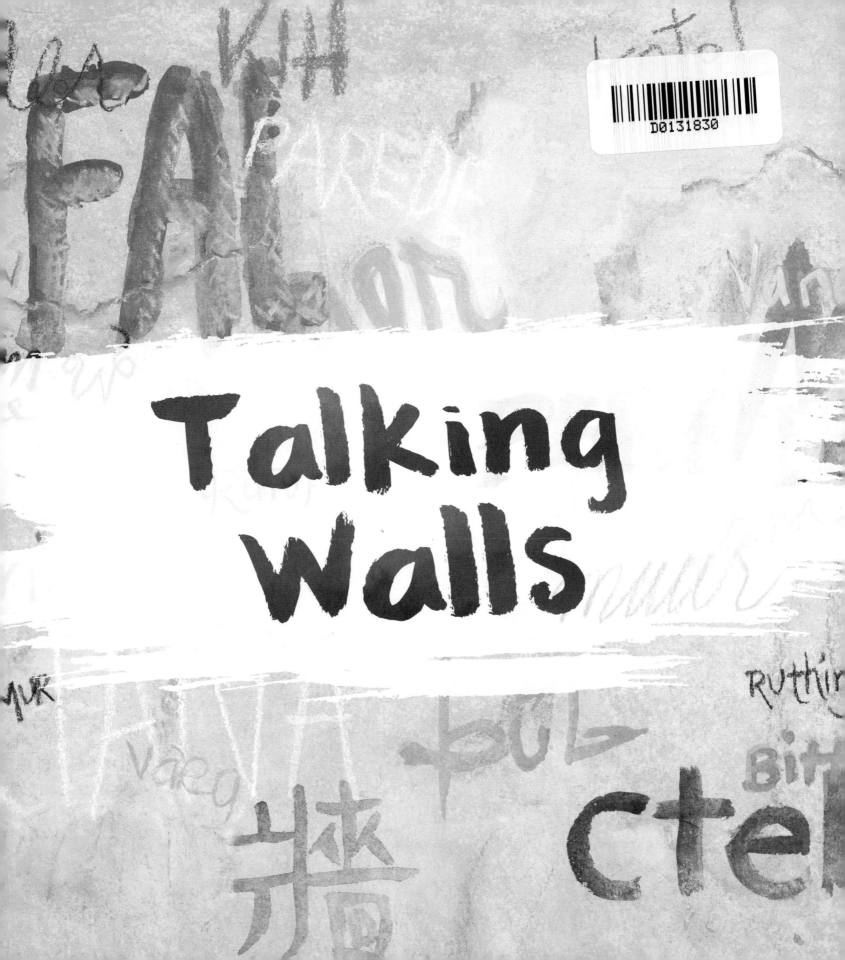

Talking Walls

Tilbury House, Publishers
12 Starr Street
Thomaston, ME 04861
800-582-1899 • www.tilburyhouse.com

First hardcover edition: January 2014
First paperback edition: May 2017
10 9 8 7 6 5 4 3 2 1

This book combines and updates
Talking Walls (1992) and *Talking Walls:
The Stories Continue* (1995).

Library of Congress Cataloging-in-
Publication Data available upon request.

Design based on the original 1992 design
by Edith Allard, modified in 1995 by
Susan Sherman, in 2014 by North
Wind Design & Production, and in
2016 by Frame25 Productions.

Printed in Shenzhen, China by Shenzhen
Caimei Printing Co., Ltd., through Four
Colour Print Group, Louisville, Kentucky

For Mark Melnicove—editor, publisher,
mentor, and friend—whose vision
guided the collaborative process
that created *Talking Walls*.

TALKING WALLS

Discover Your World

MARGY BURNS KNIGHT

Illustrated by Anne Sibley O'Brien

TILBURY HOUSE
PUBLISHERS

"Before I built a wall, I'd ask to know what I was walling in or walling out."
—Robert Frost, from "Mending Wall"

Introduction

In the fall of 1990, Margy Burns Knight heard poet Doug Rawlings, co-founder of Veterans for Peace, read his poem about the Vietnam Veterans Memorial Wall, which includes these lines:

I kneel

staring into the Wall

through my own reflection

beyond the names of
those who died so young

The idea that took root as Margy listened to Doug read "The Wall" grew from a few thoughts scribbled on a piece of paper to a book that has been in print more than twenty years and was followed by a companion volume. We are delighted to have this opportunity to combine the two earlier books and at the same time update and improve them.

The world has changed since we created the first *Talking Walls*. There are new walls, such as the border fence between the U.S. and Mexico and the wall separating Palestinian from Jewish-controlled territories in Israel. And there have been changes to old walls. Some are deteriorating due to wear from the elements, pollution, and too many visitors.

Ten of our "talking walls" have been designated as World Heritage sites to preserve them for future generations. The prison walls that confined Nelson Mandela on Robben Island are now part of a museum. And as we write this, we've just received news that the Belfast Peace Lines may be taken down by 2023.

The original research for *Talking Walls* was done almost exclusively through books, magazine articles, and interviews. Now, at the click of a key, more information about the world appears than any student could possibly absorb. With this new edition, we invite you to join us on the ongoing journey to become citizens of our world. The more we learn about our neighbors across the street or across the globe, the more points of connection we find.

We thank our many thousands of readers and all the educators who have used our books to explore the concept of walls in their classrooms. You have made this new, improved *Talking Walls* possible. We hope the stories in this book will inspire you to ask more questions, seek more information, and discover more stories. As we say to the students we meet, "Fasten your seatbelts. Here we go on a trip around the world!"

Margy Burns Knight and Anne Sibley O'Brien
October 2013

I. The Great Wall of China

Like a giant stone serpent,
the Great Wall twists and turns
across the mountains, deserts, and plains of China.
Construction began more than 2,600 years ago and continued
for at least eight centuries. Untold numbers of laborers carried stones, rolled
boulders, made bricks from clay, and erected earthen barriers to protect the Chinese empire
against armies invading from the north. Once 12,000 miles long, the wall's remaining sections are
still the largest man-made structure on earth, wide enough in places for five horse-mounted soldiers to ride
side by side along the top. Every year more than six million people visit the magnificent Great Wall.

2. Aboriginal Wall Art

Painted
figures of crocodiles,
kangaroos, skeletal fish, and other
creatures can be seen on cliffs and cave walls across
the continent of Australia. These paintings—some of them
30,000 years old—tell stories of the Aborigines, who call the
images "Dreamtime." By spreading their fingers and blowing chalk
dust onto the rock, many generations of fathers and sons made
handprint signatures to acknowledge their sacred duty to care for their
land. Some of the more recent rock paintings tell how settlers from
faraway places took the land away. Aboriginal artists continue to
paint Dreamtime images of dots, lines, and brilliantly colored
symbols drawn from nature, making it the oldest form
of visual art being created today.

3. The Lascaux Caves

Who could imagine that four boys exploring the woods near their homes in southwestern France in 1940 would find 17,000-year-old paintings of galloping horses, charging bison, and leaping antelope on cave walls? That is what happened when the boys followed a hidden passageway down into a series of caves. After keeping their discovery secret for a few days, they told a trusted teacher. Later, archaeologists determined that the caves had been used for hunting and religious ceremonies. No one ever lived in them. The paintings include a bear, a rhinoceros, and four huge aurochs, or bulls, the largest of which is 17 feet long. Painting in darkness, the artists burned animal fat in stone lamps to light their work.

4. Hadrian's Wall

Two thousand years ago, a mighty wall stretched 74 miles across England, marking the northern boundary of Rome's great empire. More than 10,000 Roman soldiers labored six years to build the wall. It was meant to keep the Picts—who lived to the north, in what is now Scotland—from invading Emperor Hadrian's conquered lands in the south. Today, volunteers work alongside archaeologists to repair the ruins, and visitors are asked to protect the wall by walking beside it, not on it. Sometimes local children dress up as Roman soldiers and pretend to guard Hadrian's Wall, but they no longer walk on it as they once did.

5. Mahabalipuram's Animal Walls

In ancient Hindu stories and other Indian tales, animals think and talk like people. Elephants bring rain and good luck, and clever monkeys outwit scheming crocodiles. Two thousand years ago, young sculptors learned their trade by chiseling the characters from these stories into the cliffs at Mahabalipuram, near India's Bay of Bengal. Today the cliff walls are part of an open-air museum, and children play among the enormous elephants, proud bulls, monkeys in yoga poses, and crafty cats.

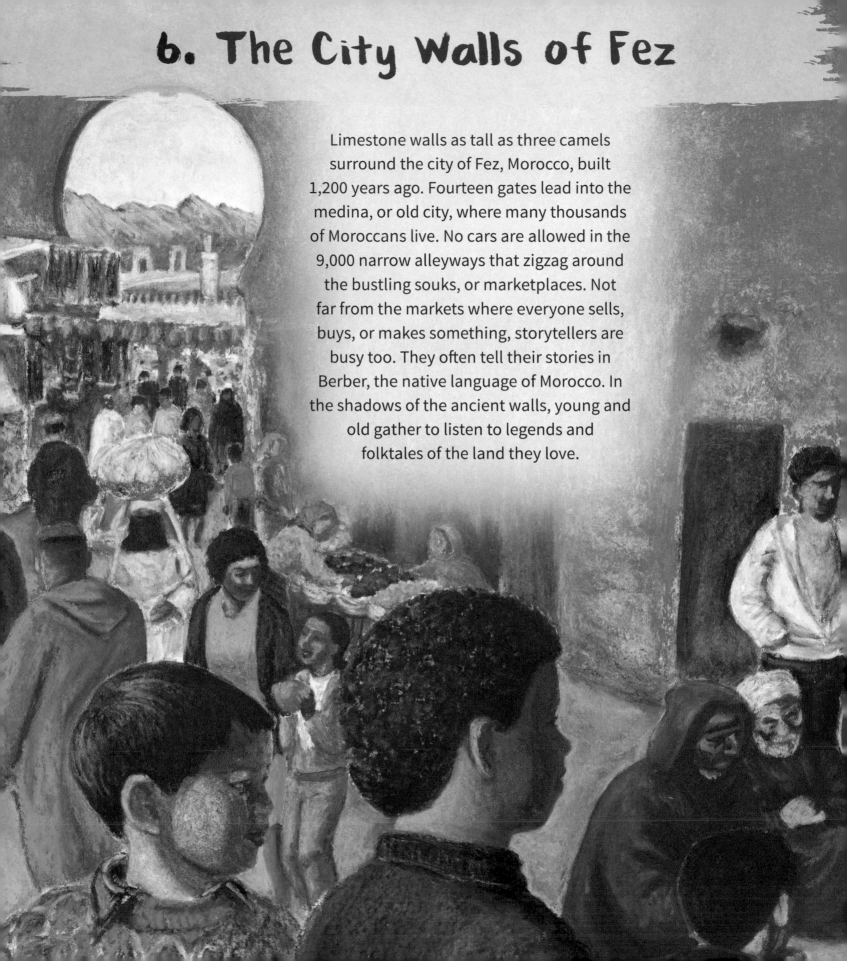

6. The City Walls of Fez

Limestone walls as tall as three camels surround the city of Fez, Morocco, built 1,200 years ago. Fourteen gates lead into the medina, or old city, where many thousands of Moroccans live. No cars are allowed in the 9,000 narrow alleyways that zigzag around the bustling souks, or marketplaces. Not far from the markets where everyone sells, buys, or makes something, storytellers are busy too. They often tell their stories in Berber, the native language of Morocco. In the shadows of the ancient walls, young and old gather to listen to legends and folktales of the land they love.

7. Great Zimbabwe

Built by the ancestors of the Shona people, the city of Great Zimbabwe in southeastern Africa grew to enclose nearly three square miles within its circular walls and was home to almost 18,000 people. Zimbabwe means "stone enclosure" in the Shona language. Skilled masons shaped and hand-trimmed granite stones to build tapered walls and towers with no mortar. Construction began a thousand years ago and may have continued for three hundred years, but the city was later abandoned, perhaps because surrounding natural resources were depleted. Today the ruins are open to the public. The use of the central tower remains a mystery. Thirty feet tall and 18 feet across at its base, the tower is solid, not hollow. Was it a sacred place to honor the harvest?

8. The Walls of Cuzco

Built high in the Andes Mountains in the 1200s, Cuzco, Peru, was once the capital of a vast Incan empire. Some of the stones in the walls are three times taller than most grownups. Long ago, people imagined that supernatural beings must have moved the enormous stones and built the walls, or that Incan masons used magic to change stone into liquid. We know now that many Incan people labored to move the stones with levers, inch by inch for many miles to Cuzco, the "City of the Sun." Every year on June 24, Incas gather to celebrate the festival of Inti Raymi, honoring the sun three days after the winter solstice. Sitting on the walls, they listen to traditional music and watch dances.

Taos Pueblo, New Mexico is called the oldest home in America because families have been living there for a thousand years. Fifty generations of children have climbed up and down the ladders of the pueblo. Families take good care of their homes in the sun-baked adobe village, often replastering the walls with thick layers of mud. The Red Willow people welcome tourists from all over the world to visit their living village. On January 1 at sunrise, dancers welcome the new year with the Turtle Dance.

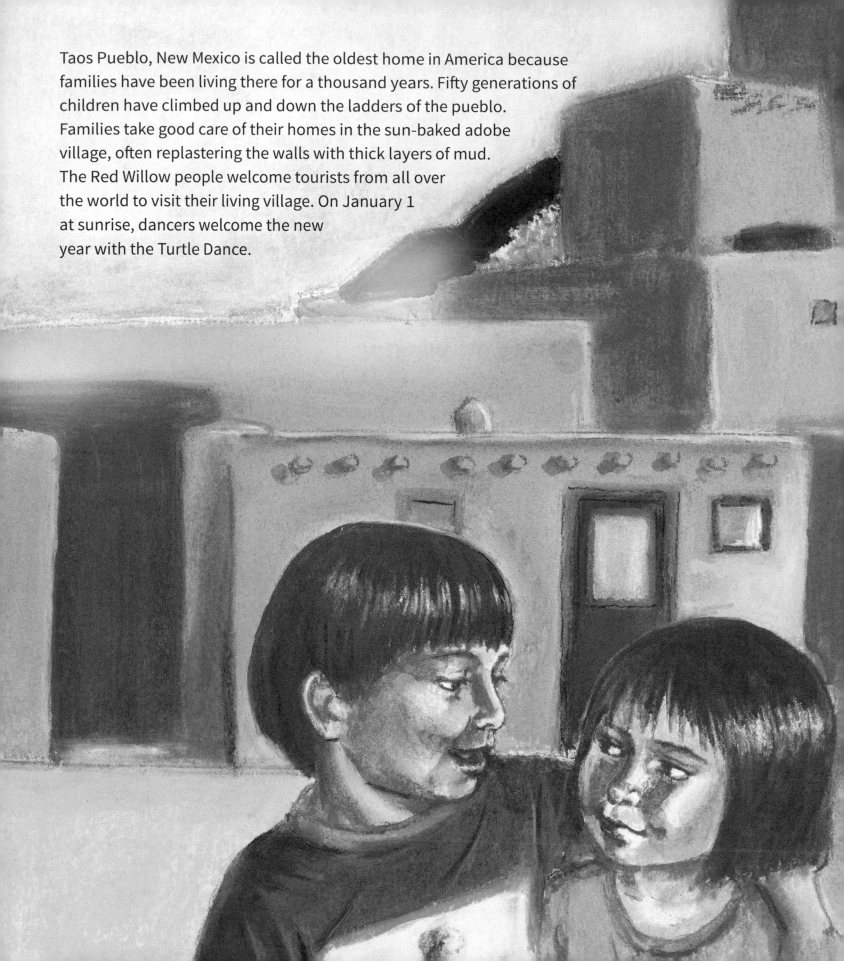

9. Taos Pueblo

10. The Western Wall

From before the sun rises until long after bedtime, children and their families pray at the Western Wall in Jerusalem, the holiest place in the world for the Jewish religion. Every day, crowds of worshippers from all over the world gather at the towering structure that was once the western wall of King Solomon's temple. It is often called the Wailing Wall because Jewish people go there to lament the destruction of their temple 2,500 years ago. Each year people tuck millions of slips of paper bearing Hebrew prayers and messages of hope into the wall's worn crevices. Twice a year, with the help of a rabbi, the messages are removed and buried as sacred items.

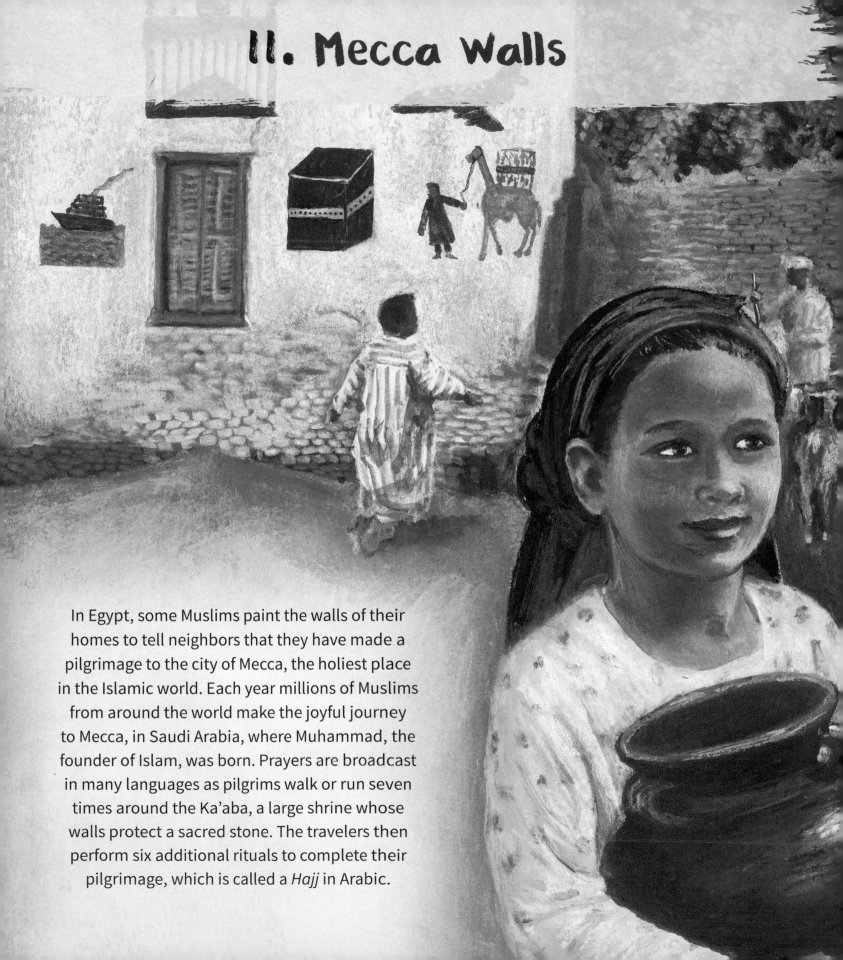

11. Mecca Walls

In Egypt, some Muslims paint the walls of their homes to tell neighbors that they have made a pilgrimage to the city of Mecca, the holiest place in the Islamic world. Each year millions of Muslims from around the world make the joyful journey to Mecca, in Saudi Arabia, where Muhammad, the founder of Islam, was born. Prayers are broadcast in many languages as pilgrims walk or run seven times around the Ka'aba, a large shrine whose walls protect a sacred stone. The travelers then perform six additional rituals to complete their pilgrimage, which is called a *Hajj* in Arabic.

12. Tibetan Prayer Walls

When Tibetans spin prayer wheels and repeat
a prayer called a *mantra* over and over, a special blessing
is released. Some prayer wheels are small enough to hold in one
hand. Others line walls near Buddhist temples or monasteries. For over
fifty years, thousands of Tibetans have not been able to spin their prayer
wheels at home because they fled to India and Nepal when China invaded
their country in 1959. Their spiritual leader, the Dalai Lama, has lived and
traveled in exile since he was twenty-three years old. The recipient of the
1989 Nobel Peace Prize, the Dalai Lama continues to speak about peaceful
resistance and asks the world to respect Tibet's traditions.

Many people in India believe that the spirit of a goddess will protect them if they paint pictures on their walls each year for Divali, a Hindu festival of lights. One painted story with birds, lotus flowers, and pyramids of rice thanks Lakshmi, the goddess of wealth and prosperity, for a bountiful harvest. During the evenings of the festival, small oil lamps called diyas are lit to honor the goddess. Divali is celebrated at the new moon near the end of October and begins the new year for Hindus all over the world.

When Diego Rivera was a boy, his father built a studio for him and covered the walls with chalkboard so he could draw. When Diego grew up, he painted walls throughout Mexico to show the glorious and painful history of his country. The giant murals he was asked to paint are like pages in a huge picture book. He portrayed Mexico's people in violent revolution and in everyday life. He painted workers laboring in factories or fighting for their rights, farmers tilling fields, and women carrying babies on their backs. Diego sometimes painted twelve hours a day to share his vision of Mexico with his people.

An Akita dog named Hachiko is so popular in Japan that a mural and statue are dedicated to him in Tokyo. Each day when Hachiko's master, Professor Ueno, returned from work, the dog was waiting at the train station to greet him. One day in 1925, Professor Ueno died suddenly at the university where he worked. For nine years, until Hachiko's own death, the faithful dog waited daily at Shibuya Station for his master to come home. Today, the lights on the Dog Wall at the station shine in memory of a dog who never forgot his friend.

16. Pablo Neruda's Home

Thousands of messages decorate the fence outside Pablo Neruda's home in Chile, thanking him for his beautiful poems. In 1914, at the age of ten, Pablo wrote a poem so amazing that his father asked him who had really written it. Schoolmates made fun of the boy who said he was "hunting for poems," but Pablo kept on writing. His first poems were published when he was thirteen, and he wrote thousands of poems that have been translated into many languages around the world. At the time of his death in 1973, he was considered by many to be the greatest poet of the twentieth century.

17. Ndebele Homes

Ndebele women in South Africa often paint the walls of their homes with brilliant, bold colors. Some women paint to celebrate a son's passage into manhood, others to honor their ancestors. One woman said she painted to tell the world that the Ndebele, one of numerous South African ethnic groups, were living there. The women paint with colors and designs more vivid and intricate than their great-grandmothers could have imagined. Each woman has her own style, so no two houses look alike. Young Ndebele girls look forward to learning the art and developing their own styles.

18. The Canadian Museum of Civilization

When Douglas Cardinal was asked to design a museum for all of Canada, the Blackfoot architect sought inspiration in a sweat lodge in his Alberta homeland. Sitting in the lodge with friends, he had a vision of limestone buttresses and glass walls that resembled the windswept rock formations and melting glaciers of the Western Canadian Shield. Cardinal submitted eighty design changes before receiving final approval, yet the museum built in Hull, Quebec, across the river from Ottawa, is remarkably faithful to his vision. Millions of visitors have wandered through the halls of the museum to learn about Canada.

19. Philadelphia Murals

When artists from the Mural Arts Program held a meeting with people from the 20th Street neighborhood, children told them all about their work in the community garden. Together the group designed a gigantic mural for the garden wall, covering the graffiti that had been there. Today there are 3,600 larger-than-life paintings on walls throughout Philadelphia. Since 1984 the Mural Arts Project has not only reduced graffiti but has invited citizens to participate in a project that adds color, beauty, and stories to their neighborhoods. Bicycle, trolley, and walking tours take visitors around the city to look at this vibrant outdoor art gallery.

20. Dikes in the Netherlands

Countless walls, called dikes, have been built in the Netherlands to hold back the sea. Without these walls, nearly half of the country would be under water. A popular story tells of a boy named Peter who plugged a hole in a dike with his finger and saved the country. Even though this never actually happened, there is a statue to honor Peter and all those in his country who work so hard to keep the North Sea from flooding the land. The first walls, called *terpen*, were high mounds of earth built more than two thousand years ago. Today strong, modern dikes line the banks of rivers and the coast. Engineers and mechanics work continuously to keep the dikes in good condition.

21. Holocaust Memorial Wall

To remember the six million Jews who perished during the Holocaust, visitors can place small stones by a memorial wall in Kazimierz, Poland. It is a Jewish tradition to leave pebbles at the gravesites of loved ones. Hitler's soldiers destroyed many cemeteries during World War II. About forty years after the war, 600 fragments of *matzevoth* (Hebrew for tombstones) were recovered to build the wall. For the top row, Polish architect Tadeusz Augustynek chose stones engraved with candelabras so that the candle flames could reach toward the sky. The large crack in the wall symbolizes all the lives lost during the war.

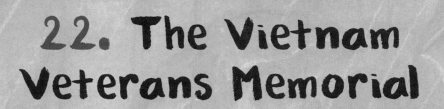

22. The Vietnam Veterans Memorial

Every day, people leave flowers, boots, candles, and letters at a wall in Washington, DC, that is 165 giant steps long. Millions of visitors have lingered at the Vietnam Veterans Memorial Wall since it was completed in 1982. Some touch the names of loved ones, and others cry as they honor the 58,156 Americans who were killed or went missing while serving their country in the Vietnam War. Maya Lin was a 21-year-old architecture student when she designed the wall. She chose polished black granite because she felt you could gaze into it forever. If the names of all the Vietnamese, Cambodian, and Laotian men, women, and children who died in the war had also been chiseled into the wall, it would be more than 7,000 giant steps long.

23. Angel Island, California

When immigrants on Angel Island were frustrated, lonely, or scared, they wrote or carved poems on the walls of their barracks. They had come a long way by boat from China to America, the land they called Gold Mountain, only to be held at the immigration detention center in San Francisco Bay. Many were kept there for weeks, some for as long as three years. The immigration station closed in 1940, but thirty years later a park ranger looked at the walls and thought the Chinese characters were important and should be preserved. Today Angel Island is a state park, and visitors can read the poems and hear stories of those who were detained there.

24. The Peace Lines

The Peace Lines in the city of Belfast, Northern Ireland, are actually walls built to separate Catholic and Protestant neighborhoods during the long and violent conflict called "the Troubles." People on both sides disliked the walls—erected by the British Army in the 1970s—but felt safer being separated from neighbors they had learned to fear and mistrust. After many years of fighting, Catholic and Protestant representatives signed the Good Friday Peace Accord in 1998. Since then several walls have come down, and there are plans to tear down the others.

25. The Berlin Wall

On November 9, 1989, thousands of jubilant Germans held a street party at the Berlin Wall. The world watched in amazement as the wall that had cut the city of Berlin in two since 1961 began to fall. The Berlin Wall was part of a military border called the Iron Curtain that had isolated Eastern Europe from the rest of the world since World War II. Topped with razor wire, the wall was guarded by East German soldiers who arrested or shot most of those who tried to flee from east to west. Less than a year after the wall came down, Berlin was the capital of a united Germany. Today the Berlin Wall Memorial reminds the world that people can take down the walls that separate them.

26. Nelson Mandela's Prison Walls

As a young lawyer, Nelson Mandela fought to end South Africa's system of apartheid, which divided people by race. Threatened by his ideas of justice and revolution, the white-ruled government sentenced him to life in prison in 1964. The entire world celebrated when he was finally released in 1990. Mandela and millions of black South Africans cast the first votes of their lives in 1994, and Mandela was elected president. A beloved symbol of reconciliation and unity, he has often said, "Education is the most powerful weapon which you can use to change the world."

1. The Great Wall of China

Around 214 b.c., many sections of wall were connected for the first time to form what we know as the Great Wall. The Chinese call it the Wall of Ten Thousand Li. A *li* is about one-third of a mile, and "ten thousand" is a figurative Chinese phrase meaning "more than we can measure," so the name means, literally, a very long wall. It is also sometimes called the longest cemetery in the world because thousands of workers died while building it.

The wall has been a World Heritage Site since 1987, and several groups in China are working hard to preserve this national treasure. Sections of the deteriorating structure have been restored, including the thirty-foot-high section—five horses wide and studded with watchtowers—that is shown in our illustration. The old belief that the wall can be seen from the moon is untrue, but it is visible from earth orbit in optimal weather and lighting.

2. Aboriginal Wall Art, Australia

The Aborigines' ancestors were the first people to live in Australia, and their rock paintings represent the world's oldest continuous tradition of visual art. There are more than 5,000 examples of Aborigine rock art at Kakadu National Park in Australia, a World Heritage Site since 1981. Aborigines stopped painting their stories on rocks in the park in 1964. Today all Aborigine rock art is protected under the 1999 Environmental Protection and Conservation Act.

3. Lascaux Caves, France

The Lascaux Caves opened to the public in 1945 but had to be closed again by 1963 when a green mold caused by the breathing of thousands of human visitors began covering the paintings. A replica cave for public viewing opened nearby in 1983. Elsewhere in southern France, the Chauvet Caves, whose walls are decorated with three hundred figures painted 30,000 years ago, were discovered in 1994 but are open only to researchers and a very few visitors.

4. Hadrian's Wall, England

The Romans called the people living in what is now Scotland Picts (from the Latin *pictus*, or "painted") because they painted their skin. The Picts fought the Romans for many years. After Hadrian's death in AD 138, Emperor Antonius built a 40-mile-long wall 100 miles north of Hadrian's Wall, but it was abandoned after only twenty years of occupation.

Hadrian's Wall has been a World Heritage Site since 1987, and visitors are asked to follow an "Every Footstep Counts" code of ten tips, which include not climbing on the wall and walking side by side by a meandering route (rather than in single file) in order to minimize wear and tear on the grassy paths.

5. Mahabalipuram's Animal Walls, India

The carved animals on the rock wall in Mahabalipuram are part of the world's longest bas-relief. A World Heritage Site since 1984, the monuments are also one of the Seven Wonders of India. The diverse peoples of India have loved and revered animals throughout history. Buddhists, Hindus, and Jains regard all forms of life as important and believe that when a creature dies, it comes back in another form.

6. The City Walls of Fez, Morocco

Fez is really three cities in one. Fez de Bali is the old city with the medina. Fez Jedid has its own wall and the Royal Palace where the King of Morocco stays when he visits. Modern Fez is known as the Ville Nouvelle, or new city. Rabat, also a walled city, has been the capital of Morocco since 1912. The medina in Fez de Bali has been a World Heritage Site since 1981.

7. Great Zimbabwe

Eight sixteen-inch birds carved from soapstone once perched on the walls of Great Zimbabwe, a World Heritage Site since 1982. The carved birds may have been eagles, which are considered a good omen by the Shona people. The bird's image is proudly displayed on Zimbabwean flags and coins.

On a steep hill, or *kop*, outside the walls of Great Zimbabwe is a fortified perimeter that was constructed by connecting big boulders with stone walls. The ruins of these walls, where warriors defended the city from invaders, can still be seen.

8. The Walls of Cuzco, Peru

At an elevation of 11,200 feet, the city of Cuzco is the historic capital of Peru and has been a World Heritage Site since 1983. In 1533, Spanish soldiers led by Francisco Pizarro captured Cuzco and stole gold and silver from the walls. Spaniards later built Santo Domingo Church on the foundation of the Incas' Temple of the Sun. The church has crumbled twice in earthquakes, but the Inca walls have remained intact.

9. Taos Pueblo, New Mexico, U.S.A.

Pueblo, the Spanish word for village, means a community of permanent adobe homes. The Tiwa people call their village "Red Willow Place." Doors and windows have been added over the years, but the original architecture remains unchanged. In 1970, after many decades of dispute, the United States government returned 50,000 mountainous acres surrounding the pueblo, including the sacred Blue Lake, to the Tiwa. A World Heritage Site since 1992, Taos Pueblo is also a National Historic Landmark.

10. The Western Wall, Jerusalem

Jerusalem is a holy city for three religions: Judaism, Christianity, and Islam. The Western Wall, inside the walled Old City of Jerusalem, is the holiest site in the world for Jews and has been a World Heritage Site since 1981. Built in 961 BC, the 59-foot-high wall is a portion of the western retaining wall of Temple Mount, one of Islam's greatest shrines. Nearby is the Church of the Holy Sepulchre, believed to have been built over the site of Jesus' crucifixion. This can help us understand why, for thousands of years, Jerusalem has been the focus of so much conflict and tension.

Traditionally, Jewish women pray alone at the wall, while Jewish men pray alone or in groups. The "Women of the Wall" have gathered for a prayer service at the wall at the beginning of each Jewish month since 1988, and these women continue to challenge the inequality of prayer customs at the Western Wall.

11. Mecca Walls, Egypt and Saudi Arabia

A pilgrimage to Mecca is the fifth pillar of the Muslim faith. Muslims are asked to believe in Allah, pray five times a day facing Mecca, donate part of their income to the needy, and fast during the holy month of Ramadan. If Muslims have the funds and are in good health, they are expected to make one pilgrimage to Mecca during their lives.

12. Tibetan Prayer Walls

The mantra *Om mani padme hum*, Sanskrit for "Hail the jewel in the lotus" (the lotus being the sacred flower of Buddhism), offers wishes and prayers and spreads spiritual messages of well-being. Some Buddhist scholars say that repeating the six syllables over and over helps achieve and perfect the Buddha's teachings of generosity, ethics, tolerance, patience, perseverance, concentration, and wisdom.

The word *lama* means teacher in Tibetan, and *dalai* is the Mongolian word for ocean. Tenzin Gyatso became the fourteenth Dalai Lama in 1950, at the age of fifteen.

13. Divali Murals in India

Divali means "garland of lights," and painting walls to honor Lakshmi is just one aspect of this Hindu holiday. Diyas are also lit to celebrate the return of Sita and Rama to their kingdom. The exciting Hindu story of Prince Rama, who killed a ten-headed demon to save his wife, Sita, is retold every year during the festival.

14. Diego Rivera Murals, Mexico

In the 1930s, during the Great Depression, Diego Rivera was commissioned to paint a mural in Rockefeller Center in New York City. The people who hired him did not like the political content of the mural and asked Rivera to change it, but Rivera said no, and the mural was destroyed. E. B. White wrote a ballad about the mural with the refrain, "'I paint what I paint, I paint what I see, I paint what I think,' said Rivera…."

15. Tokyo Dog Wall, Japan

The Akita dog is a national treasure in Japan, a symbol of good health and loyalty. It was originally bred as a hunting dog in the mountains of northern Japan. During a speaking tour in Japan in 1937, Helen Keller was given an Akita puppy that traveled back to the U.S. with her but died a few months later from distemper. In 1939 a 100-pound Akita arrived in New York City for Keller, a gift from Japan to fill the void. Nicknamed Go, Go, the dog lived with her for many years.

16. Pablo Neruda's Home in Chile

Pablo Neruda's birth name was Neftali Ricardo Reyes Basoalto. While still a teenager, Neftali chose the pen name Neruda because he admired the work of Czech poet Jan Neruda (1834–1891). He was also greatly influenced by Chilean poet Gabriela Mistral, the first woman in South America to receive the Nobel Prize for Literature (1945). Neruda himself was awarded the Nobel Prize for Literature in 1971.

17. Ndebele Homes, South Africa

Esther Mahlangu, a renowned Ndebele (en-de bē' lē) artist, has painted walls in France, Japan, and Italy and is one of eighteen artists from around the world commissioned to paint a BMW car. In addition to painting and sharing Ndebele wall and bead art traditions, Esther teaches young girls how to paint so that they too can tell their stories on the walls of their homes.

18. The Canadian Museum of Civilization

In 2015, to celebrate Canada's 150th birthday, the museum will change its name to the Museum of Canadian History. Douglas Cardinal was also the primary design architect for the National Museum of the American Indian in Washington, DC, which opened in 2004.

19. Philadelphia Murals, U.S.A.

Initiating the Anti-Graffiti Network in 1983 to help reduce the amount of graffiti in the city, Philadelphia mayor Wilson Goode hired young artist Jane Golden to lead the effort. Golden recognized the creative talent of graffiti artists and reached out to them to refocus their energies into murals that would celebrate and beautify city neighborhoods. Renamed the Mural Arts Program in 1996, Golden's organization is now the largest public arts program in the U.S. and has become a model for urban redevelopment around the world.

20. Dikes in the Netherlands

Dikes in the United States are often called levees or floodwalls. "Levee" comes from the French word *lever*, which means "to raise." The first levee was built in 1718 on the Mississippi River in New Orleans. During Hurricane Katrina in 2005, many floodwalls and levees were breached in the New Orleans area, and 80 percent of the city was flooded. Two years later, after visiting the Delta Works levee system in the Netherlands, the U.S. Army Corps of Engineers hired Dutch engineers to evaluate, design, and construct levees and floodwalls in Louisiana.

21. Holocaust Memorial Wall, Poland

On September 1, 1939, German chancellor Adolph Hitler invaded Poland and within weeks took over most of the country. Over the next few years every Jewish community in Poland was destroyed, and three million Jews were put to death.

Today there are nearly 2,100 memorials in Poland honoring the victims of the Holocaust. Every year people visit these memorials and many others all over the world. In April 2013, on the 70th anniversary of the Warsaw Ghetto uprising, the Museum of History of Polish Jews was dedicated.

The Holocaust Memorial Museum in Washington, DC, includes a Wall of Remembrance to honor all the children who died in the Holocaust. The tiles in the wall were hand-painted by children throughout the U.S.

22. The Vietnam Veterans Memorial, U.S.A.

The Vietnam Veterans Memorial Wall was dedicated on Veterans' Day, November 11, 1982. More than 400,000 items have been left at the wall since then, and an education center to house and catalog many of these objects will begin construction in 2014.

Maya Lin has since designed the Civil Rights Memorial, the Women's Table at Yale University, the Confluence Project, and "What Is Missing?," an ongoing website-centered multimedia project whose aim is to call attention to the loss of biodiversity and natural habitat across the globe.

23. Angel Island, California, U.S.A.

From 1910–1940, Angel Island in San Francisco Bay was the principal American port of entry for all immigrants from Asia. About one million Chinese immigrants entered America there. Modeled after Ellis Island in New York Harbor, Angel Island served as a detention center for immigrants who had yet to pass physicals or have their immigration papers accepted. Twenty-five percent of all immigrants were refused entry, as compared with only two percent of the mostly European immigrants entering America through Ellis Island. The average stay at Angel Island was three weeks, but detainees were kept there up to three years. The average stay at Ellis Island was about five hours.

24. The Peace Lines, Belfast, Northern Ireland

Between 1969 and 1998, 3,254 people were killed in Northern Ireland as a result of the Troubles. The roots of the conflict are complex and centuries old, but a significant turning point was the 1921 partitioning of Ireland by Great Britain into Northern Ireland and the Irish Free State, which became the Republic of Ireland. Nationalists (who were mostly Catholic) supported the unification of Northern Ireland with the Republic of Ireland to form a United Ireland with a Catholic majority, while Unionists (mostly Protestant) wanted Northern Ireland with its Protestant majority to remain a part of Great Britain. The Nationalist Party gave way to Sinn Fein in the 1980s, but perceived discrimination against Catholics by Protestants remained the principal grievance. Violence was perpetuated by the Irish Republican Army on the Nationalist side and the Ulster Volunteer Army on the Unionist side.

Not everyone wants the Peace Line walls to come down. The walls have become an important part of the history, culture, and tourist trade in Belfast, and many people who live in their shadows think it may be too soon to eliminate all the walls. But the Northern Ireland government wants to promote a city that builds bridges, not walls.

25. The Berlin Wall, Germany

By dark of night on August 12 and 13, 1961, East German soldiers placed 30 miles of barbed wire across the city of Berlin. By August 15 the barbed wire was being replaced with concrete, and soon a wall as high as 15 feet ran 28 miles through Berlin. Checkpoints were few in number and tightly controlled, eliminating free traffic between East and West Berlin.

Constructed under the direction of Nikita Khrushchev, leader of the Soviet Union, the wall was a part of the Iron Curtain separating Communist-controlled Eastern Europe (Albania, Romania, Czechoslovakia, Poland, Bulgaria, Hungary, East Germany, and the Soviet Union) from Western Europe. Much of the Iron Curtain was merely a border guarded by soldiers, but in some places barbed wire was put up and land mines were planted.

26. Nelson Mandela's Prison Walls, South Africa

After his release from prison in 1990, Nelson Mandela began negotiating with South African president F. W. de Klerk to end apartheid peacefully. For their eventual breakthrough agreement, the two men were awarded a joint Nobel Peace Prize in 1993. After becoming president of South Africa the following year, Nelson Mandela supported the work of Desmond Tutu's Truth and Reconciliation Commission.

Robben Island in Table Bay— where Mandela was incarcerated for eighteen of the twenty-seven years he spent in prison—was added to the list of World Heritage sites in 1999.

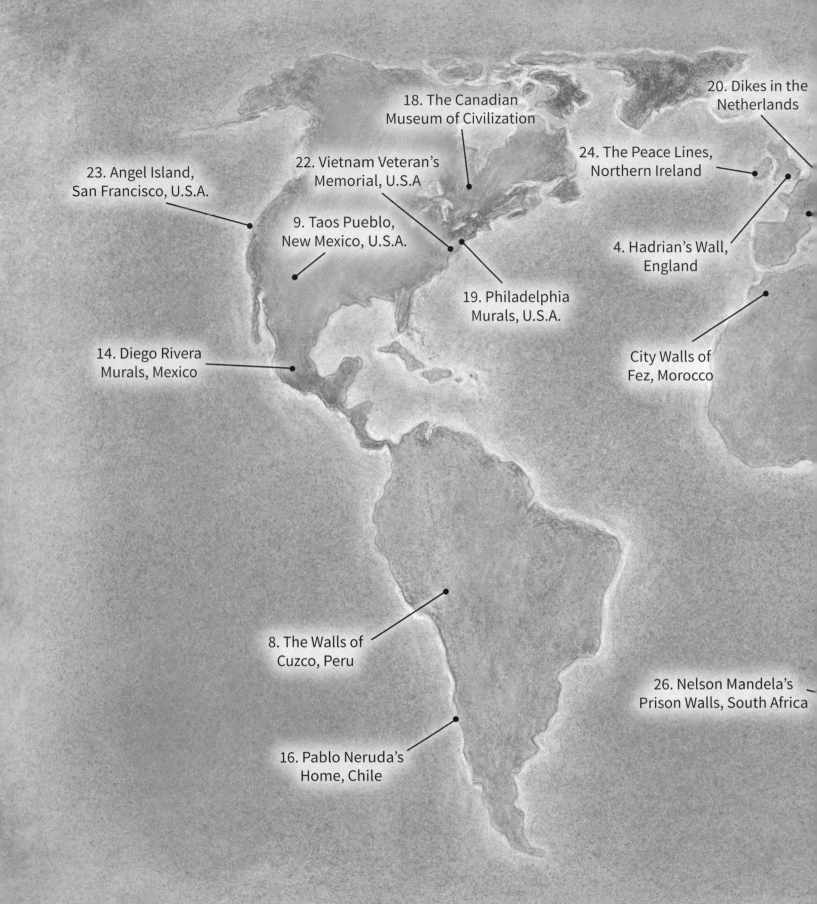

18. The Canadian Museum of Civilization

20. Dikes in the Netherlands

23. Angel Island, San Francisco, U.S.A.

22. Vietnam Veteran's Memorial, U.S.A

24. The Peace Lines, Northern Ireland

9. Taos Pueblo, New Mexico, U.S.A.

4. Hadrian's Wall, England

19. Philadelphia Murals, U.S.A.

14. Diego Rivera Murals, Mexico

City Walls of Fez, Morocco

8. The Walls of Cuzco, Peru

26. Nelson Mandela's Prison Walls, South Africa

16. Pablo Neruda's Home, Chile